This book belongs to:

_____

A catalogue record for this book is available from the British Library

Published by Ladybird Books Ltd
80 Strand London WC2R 0RL
A Penguin Company

2 4 6 8 10 9 7 5 3 1
© LADYBIRD BOOKS LTD MMIX
LADYBIRD and the device of a Ladybird are trademarks of Ladybird Books Ltd

Illustrated by Dynamo Design
Cover illustration by Ian Cunliffe

ISBN: 978-1-40930-086-1

Printed in China

LAUGH-out-loud JOKE Book

Written by Dick Crossley

What do hedgehogs like on their sandwiches?

Cheese and prickle!

What do you call a three-legged donkey?

A wonkey!

What do you call a man lying by your front door?

Matt!

What's worse than knitting a scarf for a giraffe?

Knitting socks for a centipede!

What do you give an injured kangaroo?

A hoperation!

Why do dogs never bite clowns?

They taste funny!

What do you call a bird with no eyes?

A brd!

Knock knock.
Who's there?
Harry.
Harry who?
Harry up and open the door!

Where do bees catch coaches?
At a buzz stop!

How do you know when there's a shark in your swimming pool?
When you see some fin moving!

What's green and wriggly and never shuts up?

A chatterpillar!

What do you call a man with a nose like a duck?

Bill!

How do bats spend their weekends?

Hanging out with friends!

What's small, round and black and runs on batteries?
An electric currant!

Where can you find out everything about chickens?

In a hencyclopedia!

What's black and white and can see just as well in both directions?

A zebra with its eyes closed!

Where do posh frogs go in the evening?

The hopera!

What's found at the
South Pole and smells?

A ponguin!

What game do mice
like best?
Hide and squeak!

Knock knock
Who's there?
Luke
Luke who?
Luke through
the letterbox
and you'll see!

Where do
polar
bears go on
holiday?
Chile!

How do you mop up spilt golden syrup? With a treacle sponge!

"Doctor, Doctor – I keep thinking I'm a goat!"
"I see, and how long have you felt like this?"
"Ever since I was a kid!"

How do head-lice email one another?

Over the internit!

Why should you never
trust cheese biscuits?

Because they're crackers!

What instrument
do skeletons play?

The trombone!

Why do dogs make great detectives?

They're good at following leads!

"Doctor, Doctor – I think I'm becoming a pencil!"

"Yes, I can see your point."

When is a detective mystery like an egg?

When you crack it!